der Seeteufel

And other alien species in the mysteriously dark labyrinths of the Danube

> Poems
> Notes
> Sketches
> Graphic scores

by Masimba Hwati

Credits
This publication is made possible by the generous support of The Kulturgemma and kulturhaus brotfabrik fellowship of 2022 together with Stadtwien

Kultur Gemma Team
Catrin Seefranz
Marissa Lobo
Galia Baeva
Juli Krah
Tchoubrinka Jekova

Kultuthaus Brotfabrik
Tilman Fromelt
Mutuz Al Kerdy
Ana Mumladze
Özge Dayan-Mair
Kajin Al Khalil
Luna Al-Mousli
Emily Chychy Joost
Adriana Davidovic
Andrea Visotschnig

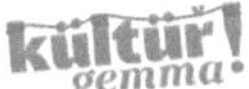
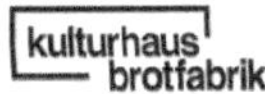
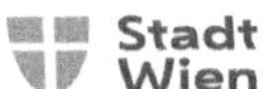

Published by
Xealos (PVT) Ltd

© Masimba Hwati, 2022

ISBN - 978-0-6397-2280-1

Design & Layout
Baynham Goredema

Contents

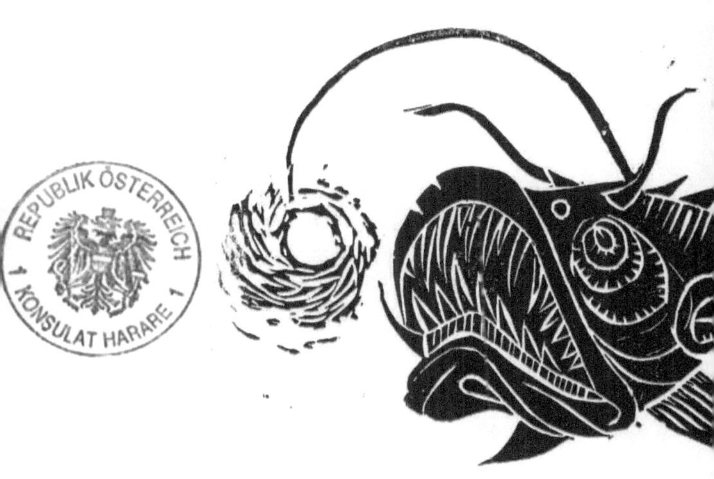

Introduction

Marrisa Lobbo

Portugues:

kültüř gemma!

projeto de bolsas para artistas que foi iniciado
na prática de redistribuição de recursos para
cena cultural de Viena especificamente para
artistas BIPOCS e imigrantes, trazendo assim
uma mudança de paradigma na acessibilidade
no mundo tão elitista do Cistemao da arte.

English

Kulturgemma is an artist scholarship that
was initiated as a practice of redistributing
resources in the cultural scene of Vienna
specifically to BIPOCS and immigrant
artists, thus bringing a paradigm shift and
accessibility in the backdrop of an elitist art
and culture system.

It is with great honor that we contemplate the
work of Masimba Hwati, who interrogates

in critical ways the bureaucratic system of
'Fortress Europe', and all the exclusionary
systems of reducing people to roles via
dehumanization bureaucratic apparatus. At
Kulturgemma we assume and propose the
importance of art and its social function of
denunciation, protest, and also celebration of
alternative epistemes, experiences and realities
outside the Eurocentric epistemological
ecology.

The scholarship is a way to dream not only
of making possible access to resources but
also to practice the politics of care and engage
collective healing and place making processes
for artists involved in the program. Here
we are mindful of affective collaborative
processes and care politics, experimenting and
affirming the exercise of caring by centering
BIPOC and immigrant artists' contributions
to the city of Vienna.

Tillman Fromelt

Deutsch

Jeder, der in Österreich als sogenannter
"Drittstaatsangehöriger" gebrandmarkt ist,
kennt den Kampf mit den Behörden um
die richtigen Papiere. Die erlebte Willkür
und Ohnmacht in diesem bürokratischen
System in eine künstlerische Inszenierung zu
verwandeln, kann einerseits dazu ermutigen,
den eigenen Papierkrieg aus einer anderen
Perspektive zu sehen und andererseits andere
für dieses Thema zu sensibilisieren. Wir
dürfen die Hoffnung nicht aufgeben, dass sich
am Verhalten dieser unrühmlichen Behörden
etwas ändert.

Das Kulturhaus Brotfabrik ist dankbar, die
unglaublich vielseitige Künstlerin Masimba
Hwati zu Gast zu haben und Teil dieser
Produktion zu sein.

English

Everyone who is branded as a so-called "third-country national" in Austria knows the struggle with the authorities to get the right papers. Turning the arbitrariness and feelings of powerlessness experienced in this bureaucratic system into an artistic production can, on the one hand, encourage others to see their own paperwork struggle from a different perspective and, on the other hand, sensitize others to this issue. We must not give up hope that the behavior of these inglorious authorities will change somewhat.

The Kulturhaus Brotfabrik is grateful to host the incredibly versatile artist Masimba Hwati, and to be part of this production.

At Ease

Can you hear the trembling Paper?
Can you hear the path of your listening?
Can you hear the way in which you listen?
Can you hear the salt in the atmosphere?
Galaxies of salty sweat, self-forming crystals
making constellations of anxiety and fear,
sprinkled like stars in a dark velvet abyss

To those who are at ease in the lands of
the Habsburg Crown, under the glorious
imperial shadows of an old shivering
monarchy.
To Milk stout Kings in Ivory and orange
gardens
Papers are neutral, blank and trivial
To the Ottakringer hordes ever sheltered
evergreen.
To those who are neither oppressed nor
liberated by them, Papers hold no meaning.
Amongst medicine kindred and auslanders,
the kind cured and dis-eased by flight and
fight, Papers vibrate in the key of exclusion
and Inclusion.

Out of the chaotic cosmos of strugglers,
comes an invitation to listen, to those who
listen from nowhere,
There is a place-non-place here,
A floating geography where Paper is zero soft,
razor sharp.
Where time is old and Grumpy and does not
speak English with a frozen shiny serpentine
stone for a heart
The invitation is to walk through a dark
cryptic maze, evading proud and rude ghost
sentries who guard the old bureaucratic
obelisk with esoterica and mystery

To All those who are at ease, the edge of the
paper is innocent but for us who flee and fight
The edge has power to slit a throat, to cut and
mark a body,
To reject and accept,
Tattooing and branding bodies forever in state
crafting rituals.
The earth is not at ease

Further work has to be done in the field of collecting of
basic information on the distribution of invasive alien
species and their influence on native biota, of developing
effective tools for the assessment of the level of pressures
caused by the bio-invasions, as well as of designing the
appropriate mitigation measures. To proceed with the
assessment work the Black List of the Danube IAS has
to be further updated. The assessment shall respect the
provisions of the EU Regulation No 1143/2014 on the
prevention and management of the introduction and
spread of invasive alien species.
It is important to evaluate accurately and rationally the
real pressure of each invader to native ecosystems,
because of its influence on the native biota should not be
considered a priori as negative.

https://www.icpdr.org/main/issues/invasive-species

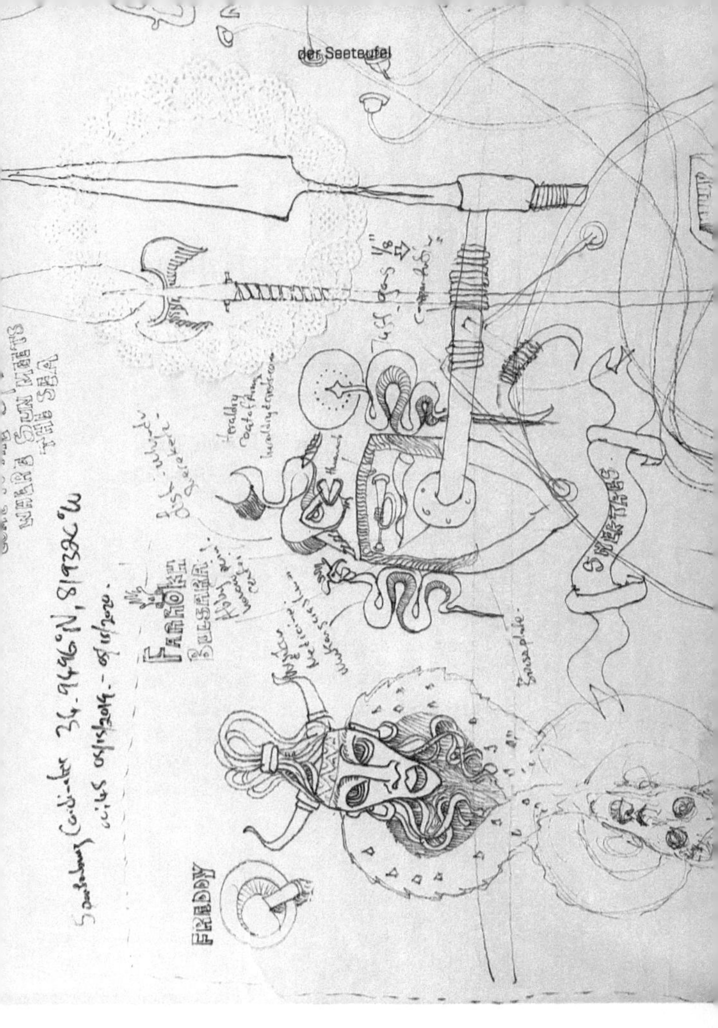

Figure 1. Days of rice, Spartanburg South Carolina, 2020

Svomho[ii] – Ghetto Mathematik

Calculate,
Calculate, Schwarzer Mann
The mental, emotional tax

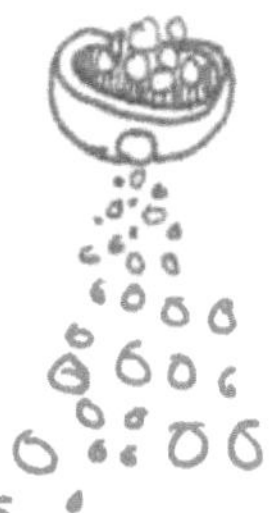

Calculate the Sift and fold complexes,
The bureaucratic eco-systems that claim
neutrality
But remember
Terminal neurosis awaits patiently

Pepeta[ii] pepeta bepa
Paper cuts deeply
Paper heals maybe
Scars are forever tattoos

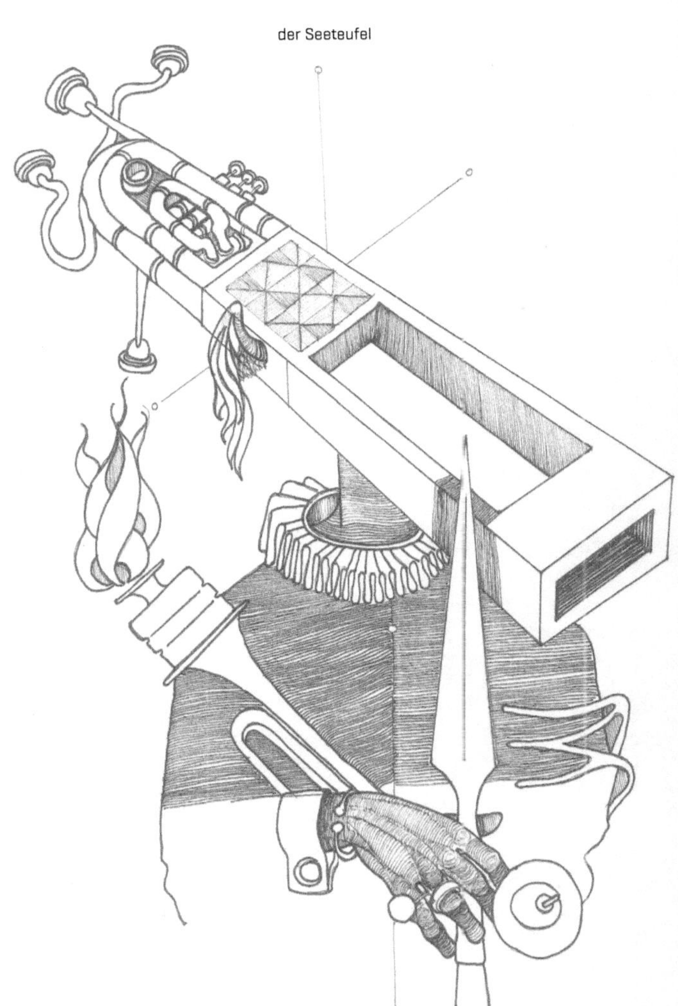

Figure 2. "Calculator man"

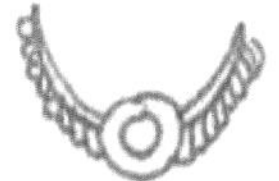

Supranational, cosmopolitan citizen of the world

It was the peculiar genius of Vienna, the city of music, to resolve all these contrasts harmoniously in something new and unique, specifically Austrian and Viennese. Open-minded and particularly receptive, the city attracted the most disparate of forces, relaxed their tensions, eased and placated them. It was pleasant to live here, in this atmosphere of intellectual tolerance, and unconsciously every citizen of Vienna also became a supranational, cosmopolitan citizen of the world. This art of adaptation, of gentle and musical transitions, was evident even in the outward appearance of the city.

Stefan Zweig - The world of yesterday 1941

Treasury smell

To this day I have not forgotten the musty, mouldy odour clinging to that building, as it does to all Austrian official institutions. We described it as the 'treasury smell', a reek of overheated, overcrowded It settled first rooms on your clothes and then on your soul

Stefan Zweig -The world of yesterday 1941

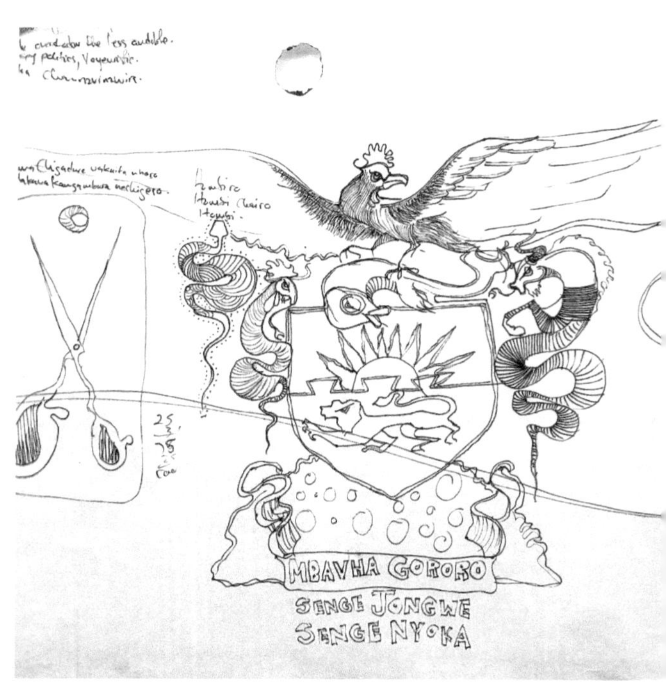

Figure 3. Corrupt coat of arms, while waiting in Spartanburg, South Carolina, 2020

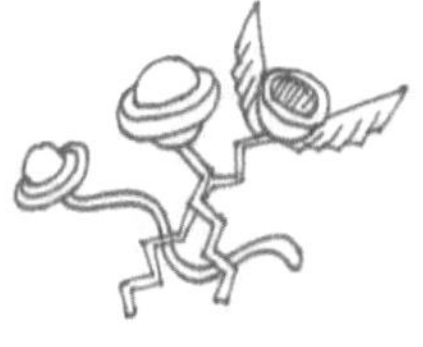

According to Michel de Certeau, "what the map cuts up, the story cuts across" [1984:129]. Here de Certeau evokes a post-colonial world criss-crossed by transnational narratives, diaspora affiliations, and, especially, the movement and multiple migrations of people, sometimes voluntary, but often economically propelled and politically coerced. In order to keep pace with such a world, we now think of "place" as a heavily trafficked intersection..."

Conquergood, Dwight. "Performance Studies: Interventions and Radical Research." TDR [1988] 46, no. 2 [2002]: 145–56. http://www.jstor.org/stable/1146965.

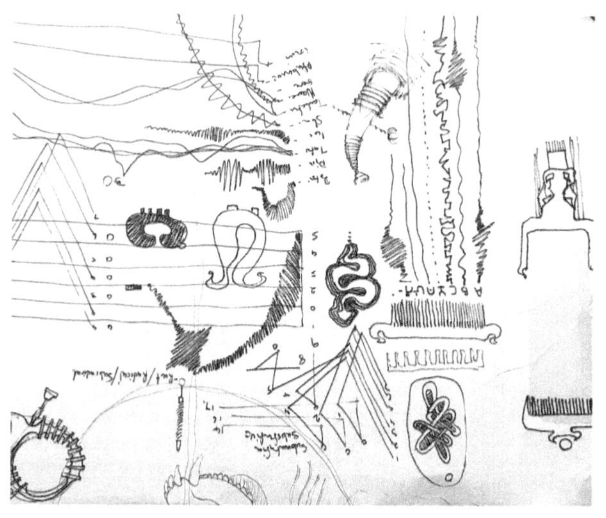

Figure 4. Score while waiting in Allapatha, Miami, Florida, 2020

Mwoyo Muti[iii] – das Herz ist ein Baum

To embrace a pedagogy of thick skin today
Is to check one's heart tomorrow
Is to refuse a metamorphosis yesterday, one
step ahead of time
Inga makakatanwa[iv]
To walk Towards the ugly monster
Is to describe a struggle like Kafka

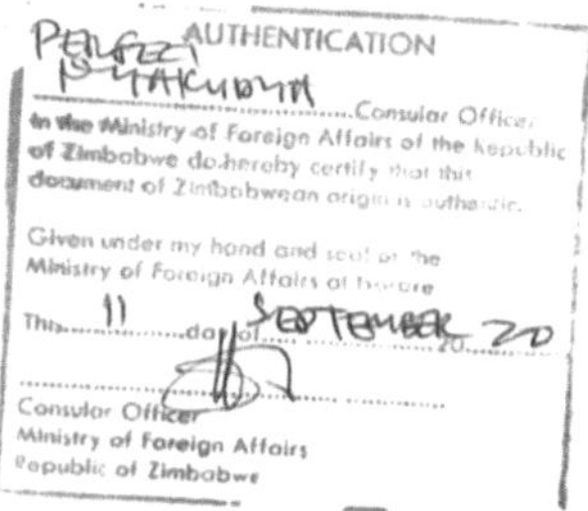

Figure 5. Apostille, Ministry of Home Affairs, Austrian Consulate in Harare, 2020

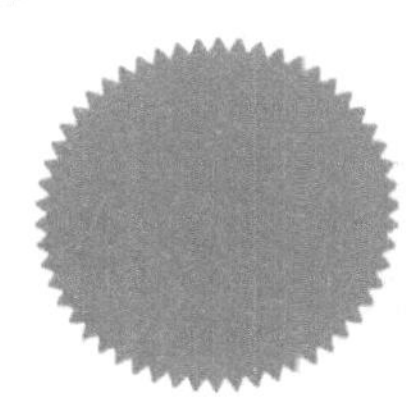

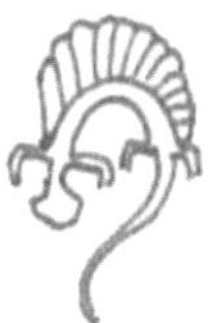

Mhindu Neshereketo[v] -Guile and Ninja pedagogy

A dark piece of earth levitates
Constantly under pressure
Shifts permanently as melting lava
Always vibrating, sensing, flowing,morphing,
negotiating, resisting,
Generously capturing along
rich soils and mineral content
struggling always, always struggling
Thinly spread
To maintain an internal atmospheric
temperature,
it keeps flowing.
like Kafka

Days of Rice

These were the days of rice,
Of rice and water only.
Of waiting for a stamp

Figure 6. Apostille, Ministry of Home Affairs, Austrian Consulate in Harare, 2020

Nyongorosi[vi]

The day was July 23, 1914
Nearly one month after the assassination of
Archduke Franz Ferdinand by a young Serbian
nationalist
The ink of history bled fire and blood on a
piece of paper
A letter from Austria Hungary to Serbia.
Hand delivered on this fateful day
The world as we knew it was about to change

Meanwhile on the other side of the world,
on the very same day
Mapostori[vii] believe that an earthquake trauma
caused by the migration of a giant earth
worm, shook the entire world signifying the
birthday of Johanne (Elijah) Marange the 7th
Messiah of god of the end times who was born
on this day in Southern Rhodesia now called
Zimbabwe.

Usandikangwanwe[viii], Urban groove

I remember walking through the cold winter
nights in the city, looking from the outside in,
Into big glass windows at warm bodies
Bodies comfortable laughing and resting in
warm apartments with the soft glow of yellow
light
Those days I was holding on to a dream
A dream that one day I will lay my body in
one of those warm houses with soft yellow
light.

National homeless Tree planting day, Harare 1992

Homeless, homeless
Moonlight sleeping on a midnight lake
Homeless, homeless
Moonlight sleeping on a midnight lake
We are homeless, we are homeless
The moonlight sleeping on a midnight lake
And we are homeless, homeless, homeless
The moonlight sleeping on a midnight lake

Ladysmith black Mambazo and Paul Simon
Album: Graceland, 1986

Kustragula[ix] /straguleshaan

I struggled so much I became invisible

Zvishavane[x] drift/Chinampa[xi]

There was no strength to go on
no ground left for one to turn back.
Zvishavane was no more

Chinampa power is desert power
I was/am a floating piece of broken earth.
Unaccustomed
Unsecured
Untethered
Albeit hinged somewhere in the ether
in a place so sure and unsure
stranger to the earth where I longed to be.

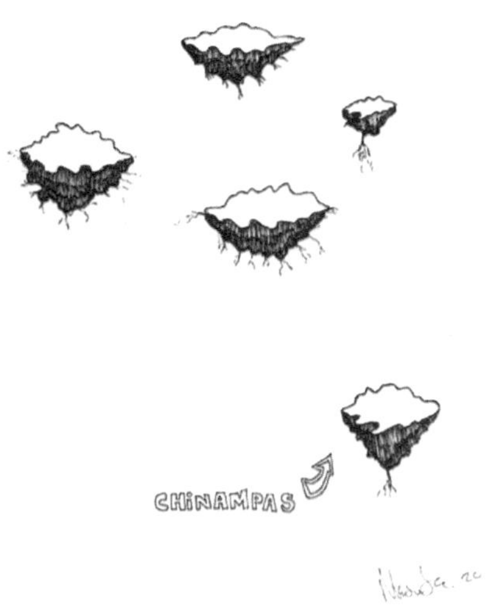

Figure 7. *Sketch in while waiting Allapatha, Miami, Flor da, Summer, 2020*

Elaborate Dragon and the golden toxin

I was suspended when two vigilant snakes
appeared
One large, one small,
I crushed their heads
Enter a pair was of Komodo Dragons
Also known as Varanus komodoensis
I slew them by the throat
I lectured the people.
The Komodo dragon has elaborate venom-
delivery system.
It has multiple ducts located between its teeth.
The dragon uses a specialized bite-and-pull
motion to ooze the toxin into wounds during
an attack.
I lectured the people.
The venom could be sold and used as
medicine in some places

Dream Summer 2020, Allapatha Miami Florida

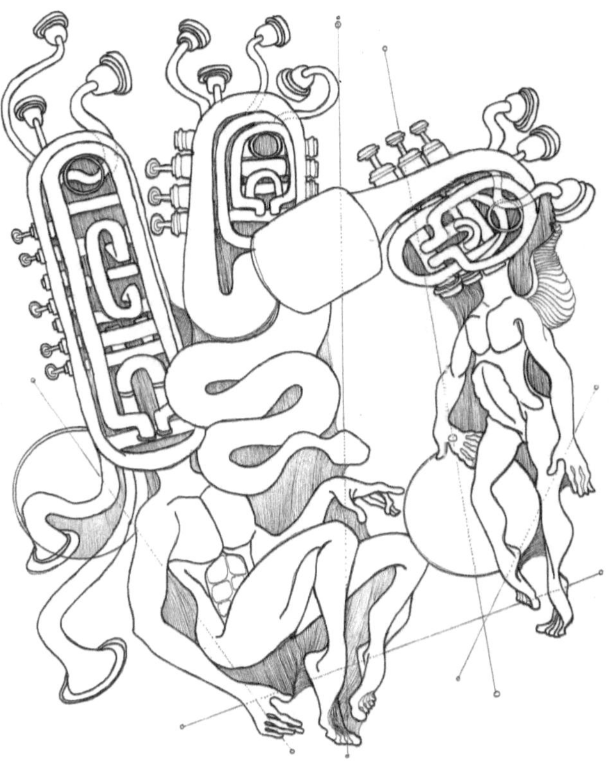

Figure 8. *Sketch on dreams, trumpets vipers, Komodo dragons and black bodies, while waiting in Allapatha, Miami, Florida, Summer, 2020*

Kachasu[xii] – 30-70% Alcohol content

With light speed
A man Pulverized under pressure is able to
processes the humiliation and shame into
some one of a kind of a moonshine fuel an
octane for his fictitious machine
Surgically removing separating the bitter and
bland aspects
This is the way of guerilla distillation
This is the way of the Mandalorian

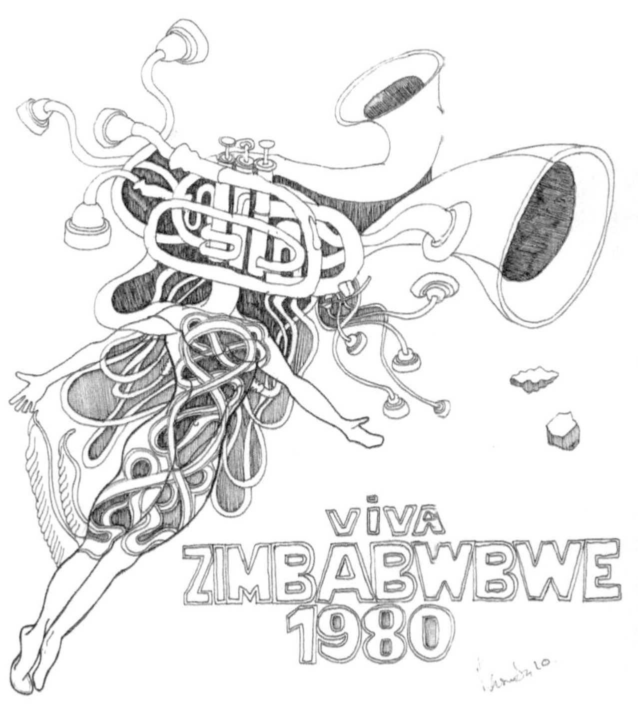

Figure 9. *Sketch about homeland while waiting in Allapatha, Miami, Florida, Summer, 2020*

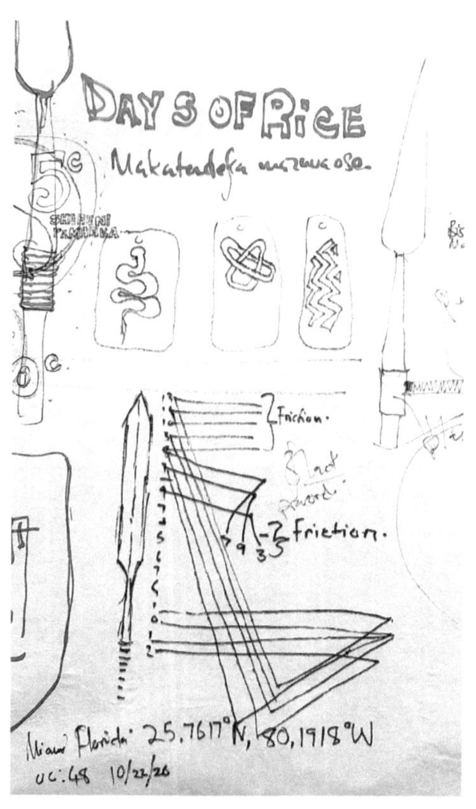

Figure 10. Graphic score while waiting in Miami, Florida, Summer, 2020

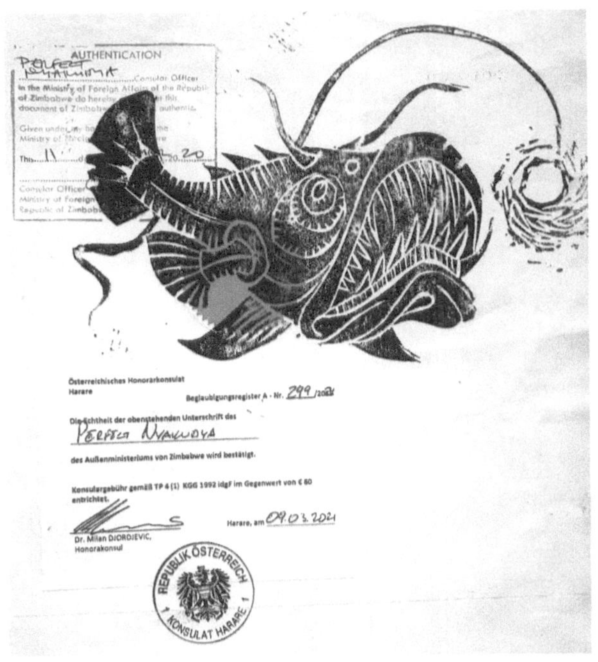

Figure 11. Apostille, Ministry of Home Affairs, Austrian Consulate in Harare, Winter, 2020

FNB
AUSTRIAN EMBASSY
13-04-20, 1   11:45:02
V:0200   R:20191214
CUSTOMER COPY
(** APPROVED **)
UTI: 7C9487-012:-c3C7-03CC-248ac-k-5C866
RRN: 38-TN01000300
Debit Mastercard
A:568601
533303******5409
Purchase   R6310.00
Thank You

AUSTRIAN EMBASSY PRETORIA
ÖSTERREICHISCHE BOTSCHAFT PRETORIA
454A Fehrsen Street, Brooklyn
P.O.Box 95572, Waterkloof
Tel: 012 4529 155, Fax: 012
e-mail: pretoria-ob@bmeia

EMPFANGSBESTÄTIGUNG

.... erhalten von ...Musingwin...
für ... AT
Unterschrift: ...Schönberr...   Datum ...

Figure 12. Bureaucratic Specimen 1 - Pretoria, South Africa, Winter, 2020

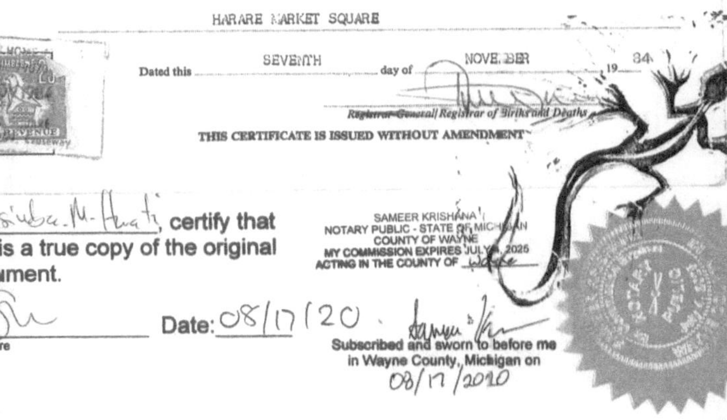

Figure 13. *Bureaucratic Specimen 2-Warren, Wayne County, Michigan, USA*

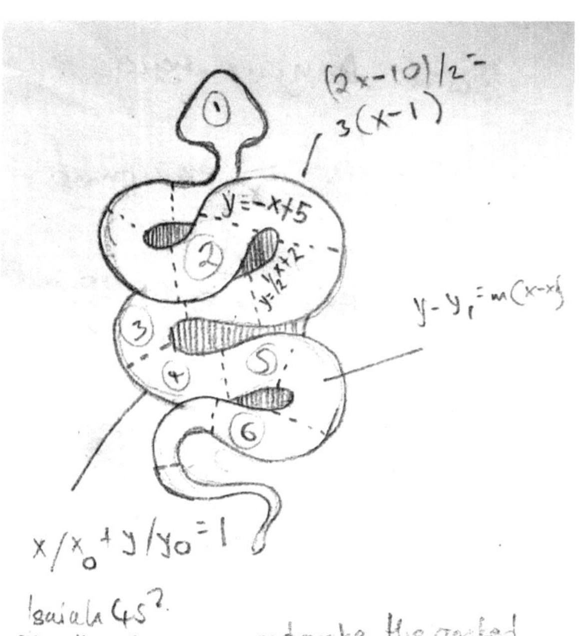

Figure 14. Immigration snake, Miami, Florida, 2020

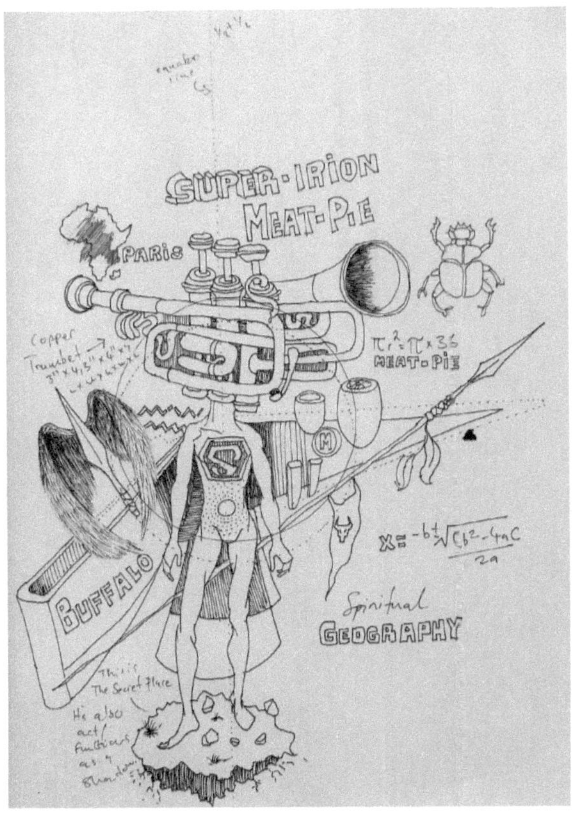

Figure 15. *Super Iron Meat pie, Spartanburg, South Carolina, 2019*

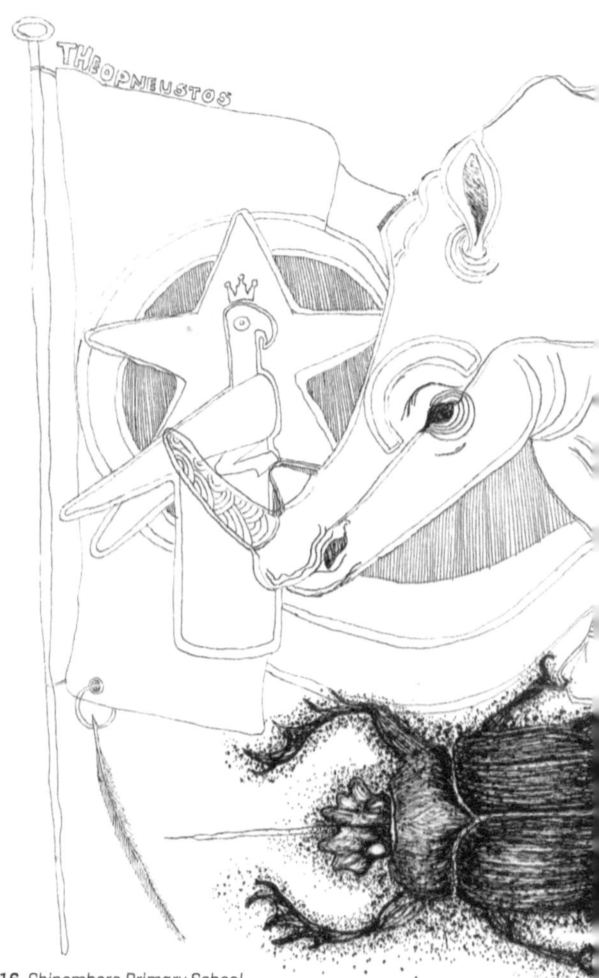

Figure 16. Chipembere Primary School

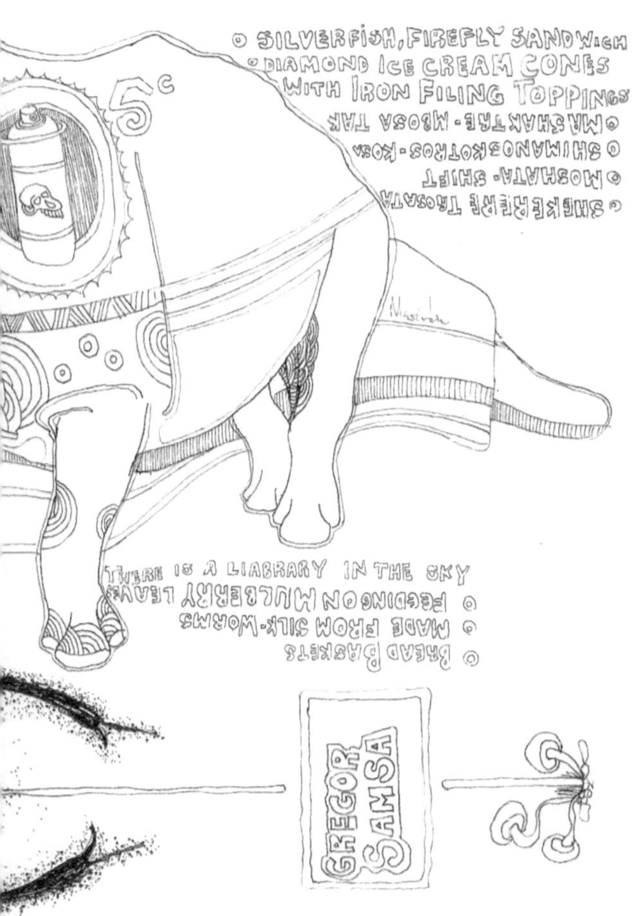
○ SILVERFISH, FIREFLY SANDWICH
○ DIAMOND ICE CREAM CONES
WITH IRON FILING TOPPINGS
○ MASHAKTAE - MBOSA TAR
○ SHIMANO=KOTROS-KOSA
○ MOSHATA-SHIFT
○ SHEKERE TAOSATA
THERE IS A LIABRARY IN THE SKY
○ FEEDING ON MULBERRY LEAVES
○ MADE FROM SILK-WORMS
○ BREAD BASKETS
GREGOR SAMSA

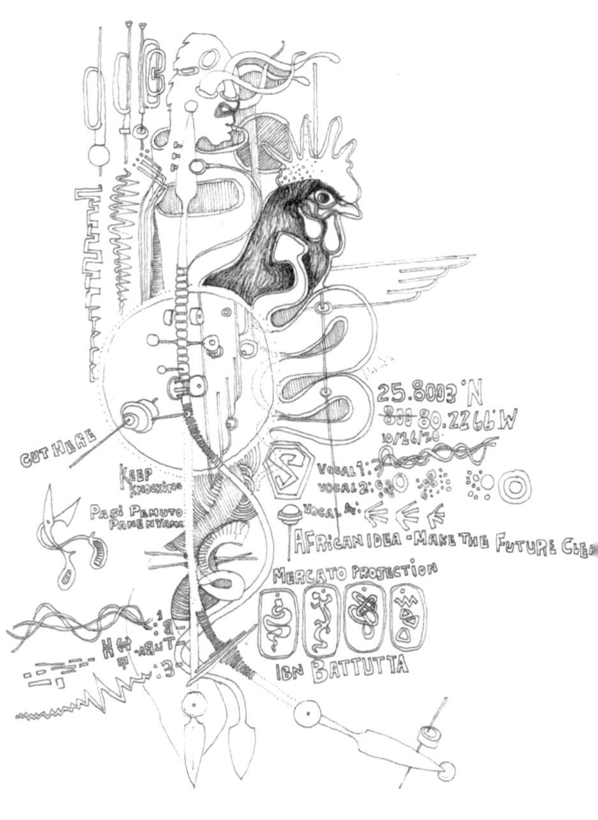

Figure 17. *African idea, make the future clear, Allapatha, Miami,* **2020**

Endnotes

i   Shona for mathematics includes the science of numbers with an emphasis on interrelations, abstractions, complexities and how they connect to everyday pragmatic life

ii   Grain winnowing using a Tswanda or Rusero [Types of broad baskets designed for this purpose]

iii   Shona proverb - the heart is a tree that grows where it pleases

iv   Shona for tensions

v   Guile and magic like skill

vi   Earth worm

vii   Apostles" or "Mapostori". Is a Zimbabwean religious Cult deriving their teachings from the bible and attach greater emphasis on prophecy, demonstration of power, and fasting in the wilderness mixed with other mystical doctrines and practice

viii   2007 -A song by Rockford Josphat

ix   Slang for struggle

x   Zvishavane known until 1982 as Shabani is a mining town in Midlands Province, Zimbabwe.

xi   [in Mesoamerica] a long and narrow floating field on a shallow lake bed, artificially built up by layering soil, sediment, and decaying vegetation and used, especially by the Aztecs, to grow crops.

xii   Kachasu is a moonshine alcoholic beverage. t is made in Zambia, Zimbabwe, DR Congo and Malawi, mainly in rural parts and poor urban suburbs. It is normally brewed from maize, though finger millet and various fruits like banana peels can also be used. The alcohol content of kachasu can vary significantly, depending on the strength of the brew. Studies have found an alcohol content ranging from 20 to 30% up to as high as 70%.

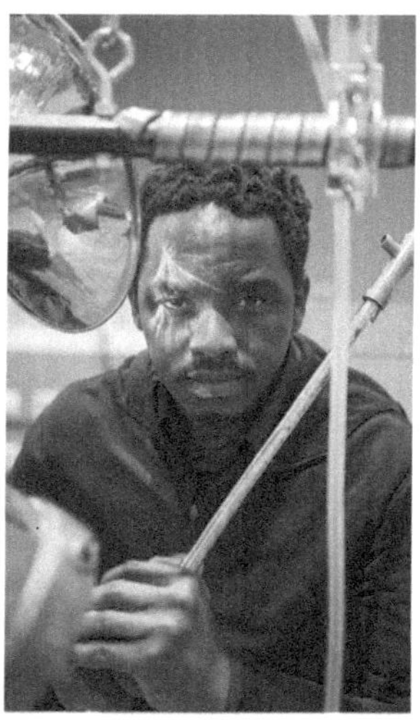

PHOTO: © AKASH DEWAN

Masimba Hwati was born in 1982 in Harare, 2 years following Zimbabwe's Independence from the British crown. Talk about sonic envelopes, In that year Juluka released *'Scatterlings of Africa'* a hit song inspiring phantasms of exotic gaze(s) against a backdrop of a brutal Apartheid system in South Africa. This year also, Toto released the song, *'Africa'*. This is also the year Michael Jackson released the song *'Human Nature'* and Bhundu boys released the single *'Uneshuwa Here'*? Later that year going into 1983, The new Zimbabwean Government unleashed *'Gukurahundi'* The ethnic cleansing genocide in the southern part of the country. Masimba's work is preoccupied with sound, listening, micro-politics, resistance and negotiation. He's created projects in Harare, Detroit, Johannesburg, Capetown, Blackburn, UK, Vienna, Weimar, South Carolina, Leeds UK and Nova Scotia.